Mirando a las plantas con un científico

Looking at Plants with a Scientist

Patricia J. Murphy

Enslow Elementary
an imprint of
Enslow Publishers, Inc.
40 Industrial Road
Box 398
Berkeley Heights, NJ 07922
USA

Contents

Contenido

Words to Know / Palabras a conocer

botany (BAH tuh nee)—The study of plants.

botanist (BAH tuh nist)—Someone who studies plants.

disease (dih ZEEZ)—A sickness. Germs or viruses may cause disease.

fuel (FYOOL)—A material used to make power or heat.

medicine (MEH dih sin)—A drug that is used to treat a disease.

microscope (MYE kroh skohp)—An instrument that makes small objects or details look bigger.

la botánica—El estudio de las plantas.

el botánico—Una persona que estudia las plantas.

la enfermedad—Una afección. Los gérmenes o los virus pueden causar una enfermedad.

el combustible—Un material que se usa para generar energía o calor.

la medicina—Un fármaco que se usa para tratar una enfermedad.

el microscopio—Un instrumento que hace que los objetos pequeños o los detalles se vean más grandes.

Plants are everywhere!

Many important things come from plants. Without plants, you could not live. The study of plants is called botany.

¡Hay plantas en todos lados!

Muchas cosas importantes provienen de las plantas. Sin las plantas, no podrías vivir. El estudio de las plantas se llama botánica.

What is a botanist?

Botanists are scientists who study plants. They ask questions about plants.

¿Qué es un botánico?

Los botánicos son científicos que estudian las plantas. Hacen preguntas acerca de las plantas.

4

Botanists use their eyes, ears, noses, and hands to learn more about plants. They look at plants. They smell and touch plants!

Los botánicos usan los ojos, los oídos, la nariz y las manos para aprender más acerca de las plantas. Miran las plantas. ¡Huelen y tocan las plantas!

Meet Peter Raven.

He is a botanist. He runs the Missouri Botanical Garden. The garden is like a zoo for plants.

Él es Peter Raven.

Es botánico. Él está a cargo del Jardín Botánico de Missouri. El jardín es como un zoológico para las plantas.

Scientist Peter teaches people to value all plants. He wants people to understand and take care of them.

El científico Peter le enseña a la gente cómo valorar todas las plantas. Quiere que las personas las entiendan y las cuiden.

Where do botanists work?

Some botanists work outdoors. They may work in fields, forests, or gardens.

¿Dónde trabajan los botánicos?

Algunos botánicos trabajan al aire libre. Pueden trabajar en campos, bosques o jardines.

Other botanists work indoors. They may work in labs, offices, or schools.

Otros botánicos trabajan bajo techo. Pueden trabajar en laboratorios, oficinas o escuelas.

A scientist looks at plant samples in the lab. / Un científico mira muestras de plantas en el laboratorio.

9

How do botanists study plants?

Botanists gather plants from around the world. They look at the plants under microscopes. They store the plants in special books to keep them safe and dry.

¿Cómo estudian los botánicos las plantas?

Los botánicos recolectan plantas de todo el mundo. Analizan las plantas bajo microscopios. Guardan las plantas en libros especiales para protegerlas y mantenerlas secas.

Botanists put new facts about plants into computers. Computers and the Internet help botanists share these facts.

Los botánicos escriben datos nuevos sobre las plantas en computadoras. Las computadoras y la Internet ayudan a los botánicos a compartir estos datos.

A plant sample should have flowers, fruits, and leaves. The plant is placed in newspaper and then dried. / Una muestra de planta debe tener flores, frutos y hojas. La planta se coloca en periódico y luego se seca.

How do botanists keep track of plants?

Botanists put plants into groups. Plants that are alike are put in the same group. These groups help botanists keep track of the world's plants.

¿Cómo llevan los botánicos un registro de las plantas?

Los botánicos ponen las plantas en grupos. Las plantas que se parecen se ponen en el mismo grupo. Estos grupos ayudan a los botánicos a llevar un registro de las plantas del mundo.

There are over 350,000 types of plants.
Botanists find more every day.

Existen más de 350,000 tipos de plantas.
Los botánicos encuentran más cada día.

What are the parts of a plant?

Most plants have flowers, leaves, stems, roots, and seeds. Food and wood come from these plant parts.

¿Cuáles son las partes de una planta?

La mayoría de las plantas tienen flores, hojas, tallos, raíces y semillas. Los alimentos y la madera provienen de estas partes de las plantas.

seeds / semillas

flowers / flores

stems / tallos

leaves / hojas

roots / raíces

We eat grains, fruits, and vegetables. We build houses with wood. We use paper made of wood. We wear clothes made of cotton.

Comemos los granos, las frutas y las verduras. Construimos casas con la madera. Usamos papel hecho de madera. Usamos ropa hecha de algodón.

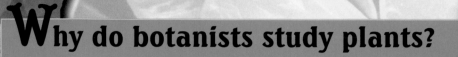

Why do botanists study plants?

Botanists try to understand plants. Some botanists study why one plant grows better than another. This helps farmers grow bigger plants.

¿Por qué estudian los botánicos las plantas?

Los botánicos tratan de entender las plantas. Algunos botánicos estudian por qué una planta crece mejor que otra. Esto ayuda a los agricultores a cultivar plantas más grandes.

All plants need sunlight and water to grow. Plants make their own food from sunlight.

Todas las plantas necesitan luz del sol y agua para crecer. Las plantas hacen su propia comida con la luz del sol.

17

How do botanists help people?

Some botanists study how people use plants. These scientists talk to people. They ask questions and read books. They learn which plants have been used for medicines.

The foxglove plant is used to make heart medicine. / La planta dedalera se usa para hacer medicina para el corazón.

¿Cómo ayudan los botánicos a la gente?

Algunos botánicos estudian la forma en que las personas usan las plantas. Estos científicos hablan con las personas. Hacen preguntas y leen libros. Aprenden cuáles plantas han sido utilizadas para hacer medicinas.

Other botanists try to find new plants. The new plants may stop disease or become new fuels, clothes, foods, or other things.

Otros botánicos tratan de encontrar nuevas plantas. Las nuevas plantas pueden curar enfermedades o convertirse en nuevos combustibles, ropa, alimentos u otras cosas.

19

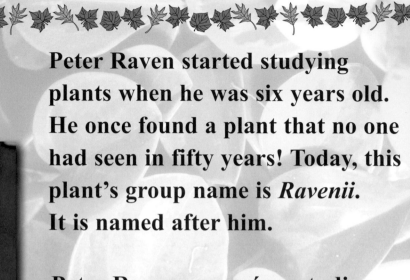

Peter Raven started studying plants when he was six years old. He once found a plant that no one had seen in fifty years! Today, this plant's group name is *Ravenii*. It is named after him.

Peter Raven empezó a estudiar las plantas cuando tenía seis años. ¡Una vez encontró una planta que nadie había visto en cincuenta años! Hoy, el nombre de este grupo de plantas es *Ravenii*. Se llama como él en su honor.

How many different plants can you find?

You will need:
- ✔ an adult
- ✔ a paper or cloth bag
- ✔ an outdoor area

Put inside your bag:
- ✔ a notebook and pencil

- ✔ scissors
- ✔ gardening gloves
- ✔ a hand lens (magnifying glass)
- ✔ tweezers
- ✔ plastic sandwich bags
- ✔ tape measure or ruler

1. Go outside with an adult. Draw pictures of the different plants you see. Put on your gardening gloves. Then, measure the plants. Use tweezers and scissors to collect small plant parts. Look at the parts with a hand lens. Put the parts in plastic bags.

2. Keep plant parts, drawings, and notes in your notebook. Ask questions like:

   - ✔ What sizes, shapes, and colors are the plants?
   - ✔ What kinds of plants did I find?
   - ✔ How many types of plants did I find?
   - ✔ Were any animals sitting on or eating the plants?

3. Visit the same area each season. Watch the plants change. Try to find new plants there. Search your neighborhood with an adult. Take your notebook on trips. Look around you. Plants are everywhere!

¿Cuántas plantas diferentes puedes encontrar?

Necesitarás:
- ✔ un adulto
- ✔ una bolsa de papel o de tela
- ✔ un área al aire libre

Pon dentro de tu bolsa:
- ✔ un cuaderno y un lápiz

- ✔ tijeras
- ✔ guantes de jardinería
- ✔ una lupa
- ✔ unas pinzas
- ✔ bolsas de plástico para sándwich
- ✔ cinta de medir o regla

1. Sal con un adulto. Dibuja las diferentes plantas que veas. Pon los guantes de jardinería. Luego, mide las plantas. Usa las pinzas y las tijeras para recolectar pequeñas partes de plantas. Mira las partes con la lupa. Guarda las partes en bolsas de plástico.

2. Guarda las partes de las plantas, los dibujos y las notas en tu cuaderno. Haz preguntas como:

   - ✔ ¿De qué tamaños, formas y colores son las plantas?
   - ✔ ¿Qué tipos de plantas encontré?
   - ✔ ¿Cuantos tipos de plantas encontré?
   - ✔ ¿Había animales sentados sobre las plantas o comiéndoselas?

3. Visita la misma área cada temporada. Observa cómo cambian las plantas. Trata de encontrar nuevas plantas ahí. Busca en tu vecindario con un adulto. Lleva tu cuaderno a tus recorridos. Mira a tu alrededor. ¡Hay plantas en todos lados!

Learn More / Más para aprender

Books / Libros

In English / En inglés

Blevins, Wiley. *Parts of a Plant*. Minneapolis, Minn.: Compass Point Books, 2003.

Whitehouse, Patricia. *Leaves*. Chicago, Ill.: Heinemann Library, 2002.

In Spanish / En español

Nathan, Emma. *La tierra*. San Diego, Calif.: Blackbirch Press, 2003.

Internet Addresses / Direcciones de Internet

In English / En inglés

Missouri Botanical Garden
  <http://www.mobot.org>

U. S. Department of Agriculture, Agricultural Research Service. Sci4Kids. "Plants"
  <http://www.ars.usda.gov/is/kids/plants/plantsintro.htm>

In Spanish / En español

Ciencia Para Niños
  <http://www.ars.usda.gov/is/espanol/kids>

Index

Índice

❧ For my mother and father, who gave me roots, and still help me grow! ❧

Note to Teachers and Parents: The **I Like Science!** series supports the National Science Education Standards for K–4 science, including content standards "Science as a human endeavor" and "Science as inquiry." The Words to Know section introduces subject-specific vocabulary, including pronunciation and definitions. Early readers may need help with these new words.

Enslow Elementary, an imprint of Enslow Publishers, Inc.
Enslow Elementary® is a registered trademark of Enslow Publishers, Inc.

Bilingual edition copyright 2009 by Enslow Publishers, Inc. Originally published in English under the title *Peeking at Plants with a Scientist* © 2004 by Enslow Publishers, Inc. Bilingual edition translated by Nora Díaz of Strictly Spanish, LLC., edited by Strictly Spanish, LLC.

All rights reserved.

No part of this book may be reproduced by any means without the written permission of the publisher.

Library of Congress Cataloging-in-Publication Data

Murphy, Patricia J., 1963–
   [Peeking at plants with a scientist. Spanish & English]
   Mirando a las plantas con un cientifico = Looking at plants with a scientist / Patricia J. Murphy.
      p. cm. — (I like science! Bilingual)
   Summary: "Discusses what botanists do"—Provided by publisher.
   Includes bibliographical references and index.
   ISBN-13: 978-0-7660-2981-1
   ISBN-10: 0-7660-2981-6
   1. Botany—Juvenile literature. 2. Botanists—Juvenile literature.
I. Title. II. Title: Looking at plants with a scientist.
   QK49.M9718 2008
   580—dc22
                                                    2007011590

Printed in the United States of America

10 9 8 7 6 5 4 3 2 1

To Our Readers: We have done our best to make sure all Internet Addresses in this book were active and appropriate when we went to press. However, the author and the publisher have no control over and assume no liability for the material available on those Internet sites or on other Web sites they may link to. Any comments or suggestions can be sent by e-mail to comments@enslow.com or to the address on the back cover.

♻ Enslow Publishers, Inc., is committed to printing our books on recycled paper. The paper in every book contains 10% to 30% post-consumer waste (PCW). The cover board on the outside of each book contains 100% PCW. Our goal is to do our part to help young people and the environment too!

Photo Credits: © 2002–2003 ArtToday, Inc., pp. 3, 7, 14, 15, 16, 17, 18; © Corel Corporation, p. 13; © Peter Taylor/Visuals Unlimited, pp. 5, 8; Photo courtesy of the Missouri Botanical Garden, pp. 4, 6, 9, 10, 11, 12, 20; United States Department of Agriculture, p. 19.

Cover Photo: © Peter Taylor/Visuals Unlimited

Series Literacy Consultant:
Allan A. De Fina, Ph.D.
Past President of the New Jersey Reading Association
Professor, Department of Literacy Education
New Jersey City University

Science Consultant:
Peter Raven, Ph.D.
Director, Missouri Botanical Garden
St. Louis, Missouri